A Time in Xanadu

Books by Lars Gustafsson in English Translation

POETRY

The Stillness of the World Before Bach, translated by Robin Fulton, Philip
    Martin, Yvonne L. Sandstroem, Harriet Watts, and Christopher
    Middleton; edited by Christopher Middleton in collaboration
    with Lars Gustafsson

Elegies, translated by Christopher Middleton, Yvonne L. Sandstroem,
    Bill Brookshire, and Philip Martin

NOVELS

The Death of a Beekeeper, translated by Janet K. Swaffar and
    Guntram H. Weber

The Tennis Players, translated by Yvonne L. Sandstroem

Sigismund, translated by John Weinstock

Funeral Music for Freemasons, translated by Yvonne L. Sandstroem

Bernard Foy's Third Castling, translated by Yvonne L. Sandstroem

A Tiler's Afternoon, translated by Tom Geddes

The Tale of a Dog, translated by Tom Geddes

STORIES

Stories of Happy People, translated by Yvonne L. Sandstroem and
    John Weinstock

A Time in Xanadu | Lars Gustafsson

TRANSLATED FROM THE SWEDISH
BY JOHN IRONS

COPPER CANYON PRESS
PORT TOWNSEND, WASHINGTON

Cover art: Christina Hejtmanek, "10 August (Ryusui Kusabana)," 2001.
C Print, 26½ x 40 inches.

Copper Canyon Press is in residence at Fort Worden State Park in Port
Townsend, Washington, under the auspices of Centrum. Centrum is a
gathering place for artists and creative thinkers from around the world,
students of all ages and backgrounds, and audiences seeking extraordinary
cultural enrichment.

LIBRARY OF CONGRESS CATALOGING-IN-PUBLICATION DATA
Gustafsson, Lars, 1936–
  [Tid i Xanadu. English]
  A time in Xanadu / Lars Gustafsson ; translated by John Irons.
    p. cm.
  Includes bibliographical references.
  ISBN 978-1-55659-275-1 (pbk. : alk. paper)
  I. Irons, John, 1942– II. Title.

PT9876.17.U8T4913 2008
839.71'74—dc22

                                        2008000491

98765432 FIRST PRINTING

COPPER CANYON PRESS
Post Office Box 271
Port Townsend, Washington 98368
www.coppercanyonpress.org

In Xanadu did Kubla Khan
A stately pleasure-dome decree

S.T. Coleridge, "Kubla Khan"

But when the sun was finally close to setting and
its rays, considerably tempered by the thickish
haze, dressed the world around me with the loveli-
est shade of purple, the shadow-color was trans-
formed into a green that, in its clarity, could be
compared with a sea green, and in its beauty with
an emerald green. This phenomenon grew more
and more vivid—one felt oneself to be in a fairy
world, for everything had clothed itself in these
two vivid and so beautifully harmonious colors,
until finally, with the sunset, this magnificent sight
lost itself in a gray twilight and gradually in a clear
night with moon and stars.

J.W. Goethe, *Theory of Colors* § 75

Contents

Philosophies

Everyday Life

Poèmes en prose

A Time in Xanadu

Prologues

Monologue for Some Prince of Denmark

(Let *L* be a language
composed as follows:
V is a vocabulary
with words for love, hate, despair,
dreaming and waking, snaps and stinging nettles.

R, on the other hand, is a strict system of rules
for how the words of this vocabulary
may be organized into acceptable strings.

Let a randomizer machine
choose between the words.

As Dr. Enzensberger made his machine:
take a page from a telephone directory
and let the numbers come as they will.

What Your Royal Highness will then find
is now a language.
And this machine writes poetry
in the language it found.
As many poems as you like!

It will be,
if you will pardon the phrase,
like a cantankerous old couple.
The telephone directory with the random numbers
The Vocabulary and the Syntax:
"My machine and I."

No string may be too long.
And, least of all, infinitely long.

Although some string may grow into a song.)

Kublai Khan Departs from Xanadu

Yes every year the Khan leaves for home
from his country residence so well extolled by Coleridge,
the one in Xanadu, and more precisely
on 28 August the exodus takes place.
The Khan leaves Xanadu and milk
from white goats only
is hurled high into the air on his departure
to nourish the spirits of the air.

So says Marco Polo,
our Venetian witness.
So now it is 28 August anno 1270:
cranes in the sky, and the Great Khan,
afflicted with arthritis, travels in a small house
borne on the backs of four elephants.
Clad on the outside with tiger skins
and on the inside with gilt-leather tapestries.
In this swaying room,
whose uterine movements
cannot be all that easy to imagine,
the Khan reclines stretched out on a divan.

But when cranes are within earshot,
Marco Polo relates,
the barons riding in
his retinue give a sudden warning.
The retractable roof is quickly rolled back
and the Khan's gyrfalcons
(of which he naturally always
has an abundance at the ready)
are thrown upward and soar like arrows
into the already cooler autumn sky
out here on the northern steppes.

And the cranes do not escape them.
The Khan greatly appreciates
this kind of hunting.
Where the Khan is
it is still morning,
an autumnal morning
with cranes, but still early.

For several centuries
it is now afternoon.
Straight through
the old trees
sprung into leaf much too early
the sound of a nightingale
and the breaking of waves.
(In some other day)

Gottlob Frege dreamed a dream
of an arithmetic
where one times one made two
(so that the prime numbers no longer
were impossible to lose hold of)
and where "four" was not "four,"
four was something else than "four,"
it was the number of horses
in the Emperor's Quadriga
up there on the Brandenburg Gate,
and Chaplin and Einstein moved
by sheer coincidence
into the Adlon on the Pariserstrasse
in the same week,

from where there is an excellent view
of the Emperor's Quadriga.
They talked about the strange fact
that the laws of the universe
(at least superficially)
do not have much to do with each other.

Einstein spoke in favor of the unity formula,
a monotheistic equation
that would reduce
all of nature's relations to a single one.

Chaplin suggested something else—
that many gods,
each in his own way a genius,
but also something of a bungler,
had each one of them left behind
traces of his universe.
Gravitation, old-fashioned gray
and above all else uncompromising,
was the oldest.
And the electromagnetic waves
so obviously created
by a completely different temperament
the latest to be invented.
But, Charlie added,
perhaps not the last.

Gods have to stay on the move
so as not
to lose their topicality.

An unexpected shower of
arrows fell from the darkened sky.

I sometimes dream
a strange dream
that *everything is not as it should be.*

I am living in a house
that is not mine.

It is much too big
and has floors
that I have never dared visit.

Something holds me back from doing so.
From the top floors

whose elegant, cushioned furniture
I only seem to glimpse

come cold gusts of air;
and from below, the cellar's strange orangery,
come gusts far too hot.

What orchids thrive there
in the rows,

and what quick snakes does the
green shadow conceal beneath the leaves?

So I stay here
in these few rooms of a palace far too large

which I manage to keep
at a reasonable temperature.

During the time that was my life.

And then high summer.
Not this
which you simply call such
but something stronger:
A real old-fashioned high summer
with the droning of bumblebees, the
discreet argumentation of the corncrake that
is both far away
and right inside your ear.
(There is a corncrake in the ear!)
The sharp
and slightly poisonous sting
from the pointed and red
dorsal fin of the perch.
And dead wasps
inside the window
mix their sourish scent
with that of dry
and now completely intractable
old wood.

And this fact of existence
about which the dead have completely forgotten
that it ever happened to them.
In actual fact a very strange state!
(Purely statistically,
we do not exist
much longer than we exist.)
The lakes finally turn silver in hue
and it is not only the summer
that
moves toward its end,
also this life.

Horizon and cranes.

Flooded land
is not the same as marshland.
In some of the pictures
of my long since deceased
father's photo album,
a document from 1929,
you can see how the Kolbäck River
has gone far beyond the usual limits
of its banks
and is transforming recently fertile meadows
into shallow lakes.

Marshland is designed to be
what it is, with meadowsweet, water lilies, cranes;
but flooded land is
something else, less prepared
for what might come,
more exposed—how pathetic
when slender birches stand in midstream!
And many a one was surely flooded:
Gaspara Stampa, says Rilke...
And all the other great lovers.
Oh silver color of clouds and water.
Oh this is still the starting time.
And

late-summer morning under a gray sky,
faint scent of coffee on the stove,
and the big heavy perch
already taken from the net.
And around their
gills still panting

the quietly melodic song of a wasp.
To exist
is to hear a stubborn buzzing note
that rises and falls in volume.
But this note and no other one.
And recently in this second world:
a pair of cranes flew over Lake Hörende.
The mature summer's signal
across the great bright lakes:

the cranes' trumpets.
And if there were a falcon,
one that does not murder
but observes everything
with sharp eyes.
Then I would send this my falcon,
a bird of autumn and maturing,
as close as the hard will
of the world allowed it
in their tracks,
nonexistent in the air.
With the cranes.

Ever farther off
in the great whiteness
which is their second country.

Reminiscences

The Small Roads

The salesman on the blue bike
had a professional pride.
He knew the landscape,
even the smallest roads.
Those that went down to the canal
to where the wind in the aspen trees
blurred with the sound of water,
almost soundless at first for several kilometers
and then powerful and audible
where the sluice gates were open
along high avenues
of pines that were frighteningly tall,
that stood there like dark churches,
and he showed the boy the way into them.
He knew where the wild strawberries were
but also the angry dogs
that could run through a whole village.
And he showed the boy everything.
And the boy learned it all.
Without knowing what he actually learned.

Strange Birds Flew

And everything comes back
especially at night, as if it knew a thing or two
about me that I do not know:
the old brown boardinghouse
at the railroad viaduct,
the sawmill with its steam-driven saw-frames
that could let out at noon
such strangely plaintive sounds,
the lake with floating and bobbing logs.
Somewhere beyond the horizon
were endless expanses of wetlands,
reeds more dense than any others.
Strange birds flew
and had as yet no name to me,
but they flew like future dreams,
dreams that lay thirty years
or more ahead
in what was my unknown
future life,
yes they flew,
heavily and just above the surface.

All Crazy Small Objects

All these strange
small objects
that come to us in the course of our lives
each one from its own location
each one from its Logos.

The old pruning knife
with its worn wooden haft
and its blade worn thin
found on a sidewalk in Arles.
And the sculpture
of brass turned green
that an artist once
welded for me out of old door handles
in a studio close to what was once the Berlin Wall
in Marie Luisenstadt.

That artist was completely crazy
and could only be addressed
in *the schizophrenic language.*
His work resembles, if anything at all,
a spider. But without a web.

A small azure bottle
with a fish's mouth up at the cork
from some rubbish dump.
A child once gave it to me.

They do not speak, of course.
Nor are they "symbols"
of something or other.

They have come down
from the firmament of forms
to stay
for a short while
on writing desks
and in window recesses.

And one is grateful for their visit.

Citywide Garage Sale
Austin, Texas, 1998

Old coins and bills
Including a one dollar, 1810
issued by *Mechanics Bank* in St. Louis
An amusing beer mug with a red nose
A medal from the volunteer fire corps in Lubbock
for commendable deeds
A worker's card, issued by das Dritte Reich
to Werner Hoffmann sixteen years old
printing works apprentice
A copy of *Look* magazine in plastic
with Marilyn Monroe on the cover
Two very old planes
certainly homemade,
brown and rather well-worn
with a smell of many long days
in the land of goats and scrub

I wonder: how did Werner Hoffmann die?

Senior High

Actually it was only four short winters.
With Thomas Mann and Hesse
and Greek grammar.
And the Skandia movie theater.
Things like that pass quickly nowadays.
But then, at that time
everything was so big, so long,
like half a life.

The bikes with locks that rusted.
The innermost part of these rusting bike locks:
One of the places
we did not study
close enough.

How the Winters Once Were

That cold green streak
that was morning
had nothing in common
with us.

And the proud plumes of chimney smoke
rose straight up.
To some god who liked
such vertical movements.

And the scrunching underfoot!
Oh that indescribable scrunching:

no one could approach unheard
that was for sure.

And the suspicion that life
perhaps really *was* meaningless

and not just in Schopenhauer
and the other daring old guys.

But here, too
under the sky's white plumes of smoke.

At the Patriarch's Ponds

Arbat is still there with its stalls
At the Patriarch's Ponds even the green
water kiosk is still there
The one that only had apricot soda
that was hot and sticky
that strange May evening
in 1932
when the district was visited
and Annushka bought the sunflower oil
No not only bought it
"she has already spilt it"

"What is there beyond the stars—
and where is the land of fairy tales?"
And in which of the houses
did Mikhail Bulgakov live?

Man in dark glasses
as in the demon age of the Mountain Man
implied the existence of
another, a fourth dimension
"For the one who is aware of this fourth dimension,"
says a Herr Wohland,
"any small room can grow big"   ·

Moscow, September 2000

In-between Days

In those white, strangely meaningless
days between Christmas and New Year

when the snow was still at its thinnest
and the skating marsh only just frozen

one always had to visit Hallstahammar
where the entire family lived

The yellow bus took us from Munkgatan
and over the only tolerably white fields

with murders of crows that swirled up
toward an early blue-green twilight

It was like coming to an older world

Grandma Tekla, white-haired with the Book of the Revelation
in hands like old tree roots

Old people with kicksleds
made their way along the factory's main street

leaning into a wind that was not there
The low rows that housed Claeson's metal shops

were still there beneath unkempt apple trees
And everything was a sullen, sulky Old Sweden

with meetinghouse, rolling mill, waterfall
And the smell of the last apple

that was still left in winter's brittle grass
That was left "forever" there.

Fichte by the Kerosene Lamp

When the soft darkness of August
suddenly closed in
it was as if the lake down there
quickened its pulse, breathed otherwise;
unknown animals peered perhaps out of
their holes in the bank.
And the kerosene lamp was lit.
It was like a small lighthouse
in various ledges of glass and porcelain,
and the hot stream of heated air
must be kept away from the curtain.
Very careful about that,
never place the lamp under the curtain.
It produced, strictly speaking, a great deal of heat
(the difference could clearly be felt in the room)
and not much light. And around this lamp flew
an angry small steel-blue insect
the philosopher Fichte had somehow
extracted himself from the thick brown book
on the table,
where he presumably lived.
Circled until the flame took him.
But then the evening was over.

The Art Room

The room itself smelled of chalk
and heavy, dried wood.
Generations had carved in the tables
so that the systems of letters
intersected each other
as in some ancient Sumerian
or, why not, Babylonian
archaeology.
Forgotten gods with dog's ears
and stern wooden faces
came of their own accord out of the grain.
On the paper, though, only the strict
figures and angles of the linear drawing which were
so sharp that you could cut yourself on them.

And this was meant to be the place where art should dwell.

Aunt Svea

She lived for eighty-six years.
Strictly speaking, not that long.
(Seen from a broader perspective.)
In the winter of 1919 she was a small Småland girl
who was really pleased with her new shoes.
(She had never had any new shoes before.)
Until she dried them
over the red-hot stove in school
and discovered that the soles
were made of cardboard.

She went home through swirling new snow
in her stockinged feet
—I have been told.

And lived on, hardworking and bitter,
for eighty years,
ending up sitting lonely and childless
in her dark kitchen.

Il Castello di Maccastorna

Castello di Maccastorna
in the Cremona area
has belonged, for quite some time,
to the Bevilacqua family.
The Apennines visible
like blue shadows through the west windows
and bumblebees over all the yellowing polenta
a late-summer day when the wind swirls.

Eddies of swallows above
the inner watchmen's *ronda*
built sometime in the thirteenth century
by a Visconti
who invited his landed neighbors
to a dinner that never ended.
That is to say: it ended with their deaths
carried out by the servants' swift daggers.

In the many rooms
that are of no more use
some darkened portrait or other
of a lady in a high collar
is covered with dust and cobwebs.

In these dark rooms
where the summer day
is only a sound of crickets
there is a delicate smell
of old spilled wine,
dried grain,
and clean dust.

Novodevichy Cemetery

How strange even so the fact
that Kaganovich, the mass murderer,
and Mikhail Bulgakov
share after death the same narrow plot
of ground under big trees
where the morning rain still falls
in large heavy drops.
And the pilots from the gigantic aircraft
Maxim Gorky.
They have finished flying now.
And everything rests in silence
while an old lady
with her belongings in her plastic bag
walks pensively between the gravestones.
Like Virgil and Dante,
slowly talking with the dead.

December

December was always the month
when one rather stopped living.
One became a hiatus in the dark,
little else.
Lights were lit, lamps and candles.
But they were so clearly
insufficient
against the rising tide of darkness.
It is easy to understand
the message of some
more heathen Yule:
To regain sunlight at any price
with the aid of flares and torches

whose return was never self-evident.

Philosophies

Centuries and Minutes

poem for New Year's Eve 1999

It is short, and it is always late,
all of it far too short—
it doesn't last long
and the end rears up
like a graphite-colored snow-cloud

on the northern horizon.
But it is also wrong.
Time never ends.
There is always time,
but time—what is it?

What is time? A coiled snake
that slowly unwinds
from the dark hole of night where it resided?
A breeze through peaceful fields?
The velvet surface of water
that softly parts before the bow.

Clocks make no difference.
It is not the clocks, not the small sharp
sounds of the balance wheel that ticks
and not centuries either,
not death that comes no matter what we do.

Time is presence.
Yesterday's tennis ball is irrevocably
gone and cannot be returned.
All that exists is a now
and that now can never end.

Come, new century—you cannot scare me!

You clocks, you pendulums, you banners that flutter
in the wind, you waves that break,
and you stubborn rain that falls—
if only you could be still for a moment
it would be a beginning, the second coming

that we always dreamed of. A beginning without time,
a beginning where everything is stillness, is peace,
where the wind blows in rain
across light green fields and where no one
knows anymore the clenched fist of fear

in the solar plexus, a beginning of wind and of light
in a land that is not here but very close by;
real time has no cracks;
real time is whole like a still ocean.
Come, new centuries. You cannot scare us.

In the Absence of His Majesty the King

One day in 1907 King Oscar II got up
from all the plush, vases, statuettes,
the heavy curtains
and the beautifully inlaid tables
in his study at Stockholm Castle.
And, with slow measured strides,
went elsewhere.
His funeral filled
almost an entire issue
of *Ny Illustrerad Tidskrift.*
After ninety-five years
equally well cleaned, hoovered
and polished; plush cushions
family portraits in silver frames
Queen Victoria of England,
the unfortunate Alexandra
and Nicholas of Russia.
Here it is still only 1907.
All the dead are still living.
The gulls on Strömmen are whirling
there in the same pale winter light
as the endless spaces Hades contains.

The monarch got up and walked
with firm steps out of his life, and
into the newly woken world of photography.

The room then gradually began
to change without changing:
ceased then in complete stillness
to be a room
and became a picture of itself.

And that of the Universe.
In the same desolately white winter light.

A Men's Choir

The voice one has when
talking to small children
and large dogs
is not the same
as that at the barber's
or from the lectern.
It comes from another life
from far, far away
one that maybe never existed

whereas the voice
one has
when caressing a woman's breast
or belly
is a third voice
that comes from a third world
(green warm moist shadow under
huge ferns, marshland, and
huge birds that fly up).
And there are many, many more.

Not my own voice—
and not exactly that of anyone else.
Is there such a thing as
the voices in between?
I recall your foot
still warm with morning.
I imagine
they must be like that.
And if one could hear
all the voices at the same time
one would get the impression

of a men's choir
defiantly executing
a breakneck series of dissonances.

Walk through a Dream Landscape

The first thing was a tree,
a huge tree

It moved
It was a tree
A huge ancient deciduous tree
A linden tree in blossom

And its crown moved
in gentle strong movements
although there was
no apparent wind

And I thought: the wind
comes from within
like the movements of intercourse,
dignified and yet strong,

come from within;
and farther off
it was still: windmills
stood with sails outstretched

and the boats, carefully moored
each one moored at its berth
in the canal, all the boats
Tugging at their moorings.

In the Shallow Shadow of the Grass

And the naked foot walks in grass
and it feels like long ago.
In the shallow shadow of the grass.

It is moving toward night
more and more quickly toward the primeval night
whose sharp insect sounds
measure a waning day.

Morphica

The god Morpheus is a slender-limbed youth.
He lives in brown water,
in the lukewarm autumnal water.

But not out in the deep.
He lives on the waterline itself
and lies there like a
drowned man still alive
(even though he really has drowned)
in the warm water close to land
just where the brown straws of last year's reeds
tend to collect and form patterns.
With his eye at the very waterline
between sleep and waking where otherwise
no one can dwell and which all others
swiftly pass.

He lies in brown warm water
and looks at large distant clouds
and the flock of nervously beating
seagulls.

Conversation with the Dead

And the old houses watch over the street
with strict eyes.

It is the fifties or earlier
bicycles in an incredible hurry
And the snow is so heavy
when it clings to the wheels.

And the springs that return
with their surge
of scents, where some of them feel
incredibly old: from childhood
or even older under shady trees,

and this second space,
where we live
who are also both living and dead.

Snow Fantasy

A girl is lying in the rising dark
unable to sleep.
She is waiting for snow to fall.
Her breathing is calm.
She has nothing to fear.
When the snow comes she will sink
ever deeper into her sleep,
become increasingly the woman
she can only be at night.
Daytime often disturbs her.

The Tired

The tired old boats
break their moorings in the first autumn gale
and go adrift,
heavy, half waterlogged,
melancholy
and quietly philosophical
until they start to rot away in the reeds

To Those Who Wanted

Cathedrals and school speeches
from very dry teacher's high desks
of old wood.
There was so much people wanted of me.
I had no idea myself what I wanted.
And I took it all in.
I took it all in.
I only feel it now
as a strange residue.
When cleverness starts to wear thin
like the dry skin of a dragonfly
from some other year.
And a stricter voice
speaks from muscles and marrow:

Someone talks rather like a corporal
in midbattle
and says:

*There is absolutely no
use for that now.*

Das asketische Ideal

All those
that wash themselves in sand—
desert birds, bedouins, hermits,
I cannot list them all—
must miss out on something.
What? Not that which is in flux.
Nor that which stays.

The chill? The purity?

Landscapes Mental States

No landscapes are mental states
But some mental states are landscapes
There is one that looks like
the land west of Pecos
Completely flat as far as the eye can see
with innumerable shrubs and a few
small black goats
that in some strange way
manage to rip small bitter leaves
from their thorny branches

Of Course Superman Is Clark Kent

in memory of W.V.O. Quine, Harvard, who passed away on
Christmas Day 2000

For Bertrand Russell and quite a while after
this thing about *existence* was not so complicated.
Existence was a crow
that came flying when one needed it,
a reversed *E*
which said that something
that called itself *x* was a value
of a variable. Which was often called *f*.
$\exists x(fx)$: there is an *x* which is *f*
$\neg\exists x(fx)$: it is not the case that there is an *x* which is *f*.
Using this method one could demonstrate that
it is not the case that someone is now king of France
and bald.
So this assertion does not become meaningless
but false.

Using this method it is easy to prove
both that Mr. Pickwick is a girl
(because it is not the case that he is a man)
and
that Clark Kent is not Superman.

"To be is to be the value of a variable,"
said the great Quine, who always
greeted me so kindly at the tobacconist's
on Harvard Square.

Did we really *believe* all this
in my youth?
Or did we just pretend?
So what are we to do with Clark Kent?

Surely everybody knows that
Clark Kent is Superman?
Not to mention
the poor *Universe*
that goes around alone
looking in vain for
its variable to be a value on.

Exit Dr. Quine,
and flights of angels sing thee to thy rest.

But back to our question:

What does all this about existing mean?

Tennis balls return,
but not yesterday's tennis ball
only *this one.*
For there is only one tennis ball,
precisely *this one,*
and there has never been another one.

I biked along the river Isis, walled in
by greenery, past all the locks,
one early summer evening in '57
with the Danish philosopher Søren Nordentoft
who wanted to maintain that for Heidegger
existence is something completely different than for Russell.
The dark brown cello note
that like a distant dynamo
hums behind our lives?
Or something else:
There exists *a single* tennis ball
that can be returned.
And there was never any more
but only this.

It was difficult to forget the picture of Heidegger
in his rector's black uniform in Freiburg,
but what he had to say about Being,
or as it rather should be referred to, *Dasein*,
right here and now and never anywhere else
was undeniably a bit more like Life
than this teeny-weeny reversed *E*.
Dasein can never be a reversed *E*.
It is hereness, presence, pain, and compulsion.
This secret thing that holds things upright.

"And quite honestly," the old logician added,
while he discreetly brushed the chalk dust
from shy and slender hands that
suggested they had never caressed a woman,
at the end of a long, sweaty demonstration,

"quite honestly
I have never really understood
just why *existence* is to be considered so important.
Unicorns, imaginary numbers still do all right,
and Mr. Pickwick and all his friends.
Not to mention God.
Of course Superman is Clark Kent.

And we can take the rest when meeting next."

Theory of Colors, 1808

It was a parking lot.
A completely ordinary parking lot.

But below the powerful lamps

the close green treetops caught the light,
and the shadows on the asphalt
moved eagerly and dark-red
in the rhythm of the shadow color.

So shadows are red?
Yes.
But a shadow is a nothing.
An absolutely nothing.

Highly Delayed, Polemical Attack on a Greek Patriarch Totally Unprepared for Such an Eventuality

The patriarch Athanasius was accused
during his lively life

of both this and that.
The Arians had it in for him.

Among these accusations
there is also one of smuggling grain.

One thing and the other
can probably be dismissed

as frivolous arguments at a time
when arguments could be worse.

But this thing about grain smuggling!
Doesn't it sound like a completely

authentic story? Why should
a Greek patriarch engage in

such a strenuous and cumbersome
activity if not for profit?

And who would come up with such an
uninteresting form of crime for him

when heresy, sodomy, inflammatory speeches
against Emperor Alexander, and his court,

offer such much more worthy alternatives?
I do not know if it is all that important,

or if it is that sort of argument
that can be used somewhere else

than precisely in this poem
and even there quite by chance:

But I am convinced
that Athanasius smuggled grain.

Traces

There is so little left.
Of dogs for example
only their collars.
Normally sent home in an envelope
along with the bill
from the vet.
Of the really great writers
some extracts in anthologies
that are soon thinned out
over a couple of decades
and die away in the ever-shorter footnotes
of secondary literature as the century passes.
Of Admiral Dönitz, Admiral Nimitz,
and Admiral Tirpitz?
A few rectangles and triangles.
Some red. Some blue.

And Die Away like a Storm Wind
in the Desert

During a long ride through the Chisos Mountains
where the grit streams beneath the horse's hooves
and the canyon swallow, my friend among swallows,
sails silently
through space and time
I thought I could hear through last year's grass
the faint whispering of the gods
of the Apaches and Comanches.
(BIZARRE FIGURES,
ANIMAL FACES, EAGLE'S CLAWS.)
Very lonely now
in their stray worlds.

Minor Gods

Major gods, a Baal, an El,
defeat the Powers of Chaos in a heroic battle

(they think)
and then carefully erect their fortress

on the highest mountain to be found.
And then they sit there content

and watch the smoke rising, straight up or less straight
from burn-beating, crematorium ovens, and coffee-brewing.

The minor gods, the small fry,
Lares, gnomes, and the little clever gray ones,

dig away in the autumn roots of the old ash
and send strange fungi

up into the light of day. They are lazy, languid gods.

But they want to have a say as well.

Letter from a Joker

Those who don't believe in me
are sure to end up in the fires of Gehenna

Those who don't believe in me
can really come to grief

"Believe in Me" means
"Believe that I exist"

But if I exist
do I really need
to be told that this is the case

And if perchance things
should be so bad
that I am not

I have strictly speaking
not all that much

to threaten with

The Cambrian Crystal Eyes of Trilobites

Oh these other eyes!
What did they see?

The trilobites' Cambrian crystal eyes
saw a world that perhaps
had something in common with our own
a billion-year-old "perhaps"
that has turned gray
and quietly crumbling
on the way

And the suspicion
that this entire lively
syntax of images
is perhaps only
our own
sprawling and jerky
movements

over the muddy beds of oceans

Fourth Gallery

In the old silver mine
in Sala there is a Gallery,
several hundred meters down
through granite and silver-veined rock.
(*For the Underground is terribly monotonous.*)
When mining progressed
to a hazardous Second Gallery
what had once been Gallery became
First Gallery. Then came the Third
also known as King Adolph Fredrik's Gallery,
and when the slump set in
the final search went once more deeper
to what my mine map calls
Fourth Gallery.

I do not know what was found there.
Hardly silver.
Fourth Gallery
looks less *systematic*
than the old galleries.
Drifts grope in various directions
without ever really getting anywhere.

Half a century has now passed
since anyone entered this area.
Fourth Gallery now lies
deep down in the flooded part of the mine.
Which means in practice
that it is filled with eternal ice.

And antimonium
in light gray bodies

when mined from the mountain
leaves cavities as large as churches.

And there is no wind here:
While the pleasant June wind moves
among the light-leafed trees up there

it is the Mountain Breath that blows here.

Through the clearings of the silver forest
move the strong gusts of the depths.

Father and Son, on Their Way

Summer nearing its end.
Where did you go to, all of you?
The boy who darkly
saw all those clouds amass
over the light meadows.
And the father on his blue bicycle
always into the wind
in his light jacket.
Meadow barns in the twilight.
Where was it actually,
all of it?
Was it ours?

Or just on loan?

The Profession

And so this long summer draws to a close.
The days grow shorter
the words a little slower each year.
I did not choose this profession.
This profession chose me.
It always seemed to me
a trifle bizarre.
The middling, the superficial
always gave applause and laurels
while that which was of pure metal
and fine workmanship passed by without a trace.
It was on its way elsewhere,
one might assume.

Perhaps it meant something
to listen to the uncles
when they played cards on the veranda
and so eagerly insisted
that *once a card is played, it is.*

Shuffle the pack and shuffle again
and the joker is left out.
And sometimes a card is stuck in
that was never part
of the deck.

Who's shuffling? Who's cheating?
Not always easy to know.
Not in a game where everything that succeeds is allowed.

In short: A game continuously played
far out among the lakes
that lie so gleaming in the summer light,

far out on an old-fashioned veranda
where people shout and bang the cards onto the table.

It is a continuous game of cards
out on an old-fashioned summer veranda
that could do with some more paint,
where certain characters shout and bang the cards
onto the simple wax tablecloth.

And no one knows where it will end
if it ever does.

And all the time the radio is on.
Not the old set there, you blockheads!
I mean a different one, a so-called "inner" radio
where four or five stations fuse
crackling into noise and interference.

And nothing in an intelligible language!

Friends!

I did not choose this profession.
This profession chose me.

Wind and Sighing Trees

Someone said:
I am gradually regaining
the capacity to feel tired.
It's been many years since I was last tired.
I had almost forgotten
how lovely it is.
To be tired and leave
things to themselves.

Wind. And the thrushes. And sighing trees.
In the cold springs, old and black...

In the old black cold springs the whole surface

of the water sometimes quivers for no visible reason.
And those are the days when the minor gods

happen to be awake.

Lost Property

Irmgaard

Dear friend, whom I once loved,
when I now chance to see your name
I recall
the iron crown of the Longobards
frighteningly aged and simple,
more awe inspiring
than any object of gold.

Last seen in the cathedral in Ravenna.
That, too, a thousand years ago.

And I Came to a Market Square

And I came to a market square.
It was in the September twilight.
Some boys were playing football
in the middle of the street
and the sound of the ball echoed
between high walls.
And there was some sort of home.
And it could have been
almost any place at all.

And I hesitatingly
returned this ball.
Between echoing walls.

There Will Come a Day

It will be a day in early August
the swallows gone but somewhere a bumblebee
left that tries out its bow stroke
in the shadow of the raspberry cane

A light but not insistent wind
will pass over the meadows of August

You will be there
but you will not say all that much
only stroke my hair lightly
and look me in the eyes

with that hint of a smile
in the innermost corner of your eye
And then I will
not without relief

see this world disappear

The Yellow Roses

Your scent slowly fades
into that of the yellow rose.
And the evening's rainlight
subdues the stormy heart.

But not for long.
There is a something in your voice
a question over many years
that is for me
and no one else.

Not everything was senseless.

I Often Dream Here
for Per Helge

The villages farther eastward,
the villages close to the forest,
Sör-Åhl and Ål
seem always to have squatted under all-day rain
not just last week
but strictly speaking for centuries;

(*Curate Duvenberg in Ål*
was briefly married when young to a Malmin,
but was not up to marrying again afterward,
says the omniscient Vicar Muncktell.)

When you come across them nowadays,
the former crofts in the forest,
you'll find an earth cellar—
lived in by a gloomy badger—
and the faithful lilac
spreading its fragrance for no one,
which are the only witnesses.
Above all else the tall grass waves.
And the Late Summer Noises:
The yellowhammers in the bushes
jabbering away
as if they had learned nothing.
The crows in the old
crumbling trees,
and far away across Lake Hörende
the cranes' metaphysical trumpets
on their flight even farther away
seeking *to apeiron* and the unlimited.
It is getting late.
(*Some years ago the main building*—

at a festive occasion,
arranged by some guests in his honor—
burned down.
It was said that they had shot off
cannons in the attic,
which had set fire to the house.)

The lakes large and blind
witness everything
but tell of nothing.

In the meanderings of the river up at Byggetorp
there is some unfrequented marshland.
Strange channels loose their way
in the mazes of the reeds.
The house simple
but with a view for miles
across large wise expanses of water.
The grass snake, faithful under the floorboards,
is quiet and retiring
but is there even so.
I often dream there
Then I resaw the actual place,
the rushes, and those still inner waters
which without any scent
became simply an eye
and the bright sky reflected
the still unfathomableness of the summer day.
And then I thought:
What does this place want of me?

But the place wants nothing of me.
And the dream has no horizon.

Everyday Life

Sleeping with a Cat in the Bed

I don't know if I like cats.
Dogs are more my sort of animal.
Dogs don't lie as often.
But it's nice sleeping with cats
in bed, somewhere down
in the foot area just where the toes
cautiously peep out into a nocturnal world
like watchmen on the wall
of a very old city.
Sleep City on the Plain of Dark.
The cat then at a suitable distance
but in a kind of secret understanding
with the toes, these ten watchmen,
against the dark, chaos, the void,
and the sound of the distant train.

And the cat's sleep creates in me
a deeper sleep,
its way of curling around its
own center like an embryo
gives a feeling of intimacy,
yes snugness, in this world,
as if it was
a perfectly natural place
to stay in.

Libraries Are a Kind of Subway

The ingrained smells of libraries,
just as self-evident as those of subways:

a smell of hot metal and oxidized urine.

And libraries *are* subways.
You often know where you emerge

to the agitated life of the surface again,

but sometimes in a completely unexpected place.

Ramsberg's Thumb

There was something peculiar
about Ramsberg's one thumb.
I think a circular saw had taken
half of it

He built our stove
in '39 and it still works

The remaining joint
had something childishly round
and defenseless about it

Nature and unnature
at one and the same time.
Or nature's remarkable ability
to behave unnaturally

Even today
I often think
of Ramsberg's thumb

The Girl

One day life stands
gently smiling like a girl
suddenly on the other side of the stream
and asks
(in her annoying way),

But how did you end up there?

Poèmes en prose

The Freiburg Dream

At 2:30 a.m. on a September night in '99 there is a knock on the
door to my room in Hotel zur Alten Post in Freiburg. A city in the
Black Forest that is quiet at night.

Not without some effort I get out of bed and open the slightly
creaking door to a completely empty and silent hotel corridor. The
door-creak is the only sound to be heard. There is really nothing
here. The knocking remains a mystery. A mistake perhaps? Perhaps
someone with far too much on board who misread the room
number? Perhaps someone from the past?

Suddenly very tired I decide not to walk but to *float* back to
bed. And it all goes splendidly. An invisible force lifts me to a
suitable height and like a fish in an aquarium I float leisurely back
to the bed, where I carefully let myself down. Careful about not
"letting go" from too great a height. And now of course quite
aware of the fact that I am dreaming. A situation I have quickly
seen through, but cunningly turn to my own advantage.

So, after all, Descartes got it wrong.

A World That Once Existed

In an old-fashioned bookcase, behind glass doors with green curtains on the inside, stand nineteenth-century travel accounts with etchings and woodcuts and neat cloth bindings with engraved illustrations.

They seek to convince us. Of what? Of the other places, perhaps. That they really exist.

So: deep inside sepia-colored jungles white men move in long, laced leggings at the head of some forty bearers. Ever deeper into a mysterious continent. And the air balloon hovers, weightless above white Arctic expanses where not even a sea lion disturbs the serenity from its opening in the ice. And out on the great steppe entire peoples live in tents of skins and distill their spirits from mare's milk that is allowed to ferment slowly in a leather pouch at the door of the yurt.

Yes, even they exist. These other ones—the real places.

The harbor in Tristan da Cunha. But never a bonemeal factory in Köping—

Oh, we believed in them for so long. The old, dear books.

And now we must soon do something else with life so it can become real again.

The Growing Man

From the other seat an enormously fat man swells slowly but persuasively over toward my side. He smells of stale sweat and has a completely gray face and seems to get bigger and bigger as the flight proceeds. It is easy to understand how oak trunks can split open old boulders in whose clefts their acorns have once landed.

The whole time he is attentively reading some sort of religious tract, which (seen from over the shoulder) seems to deal with how to hold on to one's belief in something or other, even though long since in doubt.

The more he reads and slowly turns the pages of his silly book, the more he seems to swell out in all directions.

Soon there will be room for nothing else here.

The Stationary Man

In central Lisbon, near Rossio in Rua Augusta, a man has developed his own unique form of art. He stands. Completely still, for around half an hour, on a pedestal. He wears a somewhat threadbare tailcoat—just like orchestra conductors and other artists who are used to appearing in public—his face is elegantly made up in white but not as harshly as that of a clown. His arms are slightly extended although not quite as high as those in Thorvaldsen's statue of Christ. Standing there in the elegant long nineteenth-century street—it leads down to the river Tagus, or Tejo, as the Portuguese call it—he creates the striking illusion, especially from a certain perspective and distance, of being a statue. In front of the pallet that functions as a plinth the maestro has placed a top hat in which he receives contributions.

In a world where most people try to attract people's attention by some form of sophisticated activity, this unusual artist, who has made absolute stillness his art, seems worthy of respect.

Why do I quietly admire this stationary man? What do I see in him that is so remarkable? Perhaps that I myself am completely unable to be still, that I always have to be in motion.

Why?

Anyone in sufficiently rapid motion must of course sooner or later become invisible.

One way of being in motion is to move from one place to another. *Without passing the points in between.*

The River Man

A harsh Portuguese winter day, 31 January 1878 to be precise, the strange American Paul Boyton stepped down into the cool waves of the Tagus in Toledo, on the Spanish side that is, and let himself float, in a horizontal position, all the way down to Lisbon, where the river joins the sea just after the old citadel in Beleme. The intention was to demonstrate a floating costume he had invented which kept the traveler in a pleasantly high horizontal position and was clearly also able to keep him dry and warm. This fantastic floating suit had five independent floating elements and evidently a host of practical pockets in which Boyton took along a map, a compass, and a horn for drawing the attention of oncoming and passing boat traffic to his presence. A revolver. And furthermore a small American flag with a telescopic pole, which he, apparently with pride, bore with him down to the riverbank in Toledo where, according to unanimous contemporary Spanish and Portuguese press information, he was enthusiastically greeted by large masses of spectators. He spent the nights at locations along the river, and at inn tables inquired about eddies and sandbanks. The progress downriver of the floating man was evidently a great success, and he was greeted at the Tejo estuary by crowds of people. Boyton, who was later awarded the Congressional Gold Medal for his efforts in service of sea rescue, was in the American navy during the Civil War and was a pioneer in the field of submarines.

What one asks oneself—naturally—is what strange thoughts can have passed through his head during the endlessly long, monotonous winter days on the river Tagus.

The Girl in the Supermarket

Poets and other prizewinning optimists tend to insist that each human being is a great mystery, even—in severe cases—a cathedral. But not a football stadium, an underground station, a hospital—which would be equally possible images.

Most people seem uninteresting. However, those who are interesting are not the ones publicly regarded as such. Really interesting people have one thing in common: it is difficult to formulate what it is that makes them such.

The girl in the supermarket is small, blond, her face slightly too broad to be beautiful. She is consistently friendly to all customers, from Sunday afternoon's red-faced gentlemen who want their six-packs to the refined old ladies in wheelchairs.

Her eyes do not express much. If you look into them you meet an obstacle. She doesn't look away. She doesn't blink. I don't know how she does it. Or maybe, like spaceships of the future, she has a shield and an invisibility cloak. Or maybe she has learned how to evacuate the territory of the eye very fast if someone threatens to invade.

It takes two winters and two springs of diligent shopping in this store before I get at least an inkling, a clue, as to the riddle of this interesting person.

If one listens carefully to her friendly conversation with the various customers, one will discover that she always addresses each of them by name.

And never misses a name.

Notes

Xanadu, in northern China near the border with the present-day Mongolian Republic; once a summer residence of the Mongol Emperor Kublai Khan. Ruins of the emperor's summer palace still exist, but over the past century most have been removed as building material. Coleridge's well-known poem "Kubla Khan," possibly the poetic pinnacle of the English Romantic Movement, begins with the familiar lines:

> In Xanadu did Kubla Khan
> A stately pleasure-dome decree:
> Where Alph, the sacred river, ran
> Through caverns measureless to man
> Down to a sunless sea.

As commentators seldom fail to remark, the first lines of this peculiar poem are an almost verbatim transcription of a description in Samuel Purchas's *Purchas his Pilgrimage* (1613).

Much more can be read about Kublai Khan, his summer palace, and life there in *The Travels of Marco Polo*. Kublai Khan (1215–1294) was the grandson of Genghis Khan and was the first Mongol emperor to bring his capital to Peking.

Hans Magnus Enzensberger's poetry machine (p. 5) actually exists. It can be studied in his book *Einladung zu einem Poesie-Automaten* [Invitation to a Poetry Automate] (Suhrkamp, 2000) and can be studied at the Museum of Modern Literature in Marburg. The machine permutes, according to certain programmed rules, a random sample of words and arranges them in syntactically well-organized sequences of limited length. See also my poem "The Machines" in *The Stillness of the World Before Bach* (1988).

Logos (p. 17), a word of many meanings, can be translated as "plan," "norm," or "program." We also find it used in a Neoplatonic sense in the opening to Saint John's Gospel, where it is normally translated as "the Word." But this word must be conceived as being normative, formative.

Arbat (p. 22), a precinct in central Moscow—also the name of a friendly pedestrian street with a tourist atmosphere. Here Bulgakov lived for a while in the early 1930s. Not all that far away lies the Bishop or Patriarch's Ponds, the peaceful square where Bulgakov's immortal novel *The Master and Margarita* locates its first chapter.

The Mountain Man (p. 22), Mandelstam's pejorative epithet in the satirical poem about Stalin which was to lead to the poet's death.

Das asketische Ideal (p. 46)—from Friedrich Nietzsche's *Zur Genealogie der Moral* (*On the Genealogy of Mortality*).

Of Course Superman Is Clark Kent (p. 48)—in the popular modern myth it is of course so. However, if we follow Bertrand Russell's later, much-discussed (Searle, Strawson, et al.) interpretation of existential assertions with particular descriptions—"On Denoting" (1905)—sentences such as *The present King of France is bald* must be conceived as existential assertions and thus become false. But this has the consequence that *Superman is Clark Kent* becomes a false sentence.

Since this is totally irreconcilable with normal language usage, we have to draw the conclusion that Russell's analysis misses something important in the relationship between meaning and reference.

Heidegger's view of Being, based on thoughts about pre-Socratic philosophy, leads to a completely different conception of what it means to exist. Heidegger's word is *Dasein*—presence.

During one year at the beginning of the Nazi era Heidegger held the post of rector of Freiburg University and wore a black rector's uniform of his own design.

Theory of Colors, 1808 (p. 51) refers to Goethe's *Farbenlehre,* which was completed that year. The poem alludes to the chapter on shadow colors—especially sections 72, 73, and the incredibly beautiful 75.

LG, Austin, May 2001

About the Author

Lars Gustafsson is one of Scandinavia's best-known authors. Born in Västerås, Sweden, in 1936, he published his first novel, *Vägvila: ett mysteriespel på prosa* (Rest on the Way: A Mystery Play in Prose), at the age of twenty-one. His work has won many awards, including the Prix Européen de l'Essai Charles Veillon (1983), the Swedish Academy's Bellman Prize (1990), and the Swedish Pilot Prize (1996). His works are concerned with the search for moral consciousness and the relationship between personal experience and self-awareness, imbued with a philosophically founded skepticism toward language. Between 1982 and 2004, Gustafsson taught philosophy at the University of Texas at Austin. He presently lives as a Jamail Distinguised Professor Emeritus in Stockholm, Sweden.

About the Translator

John Irons studied French, German, and Dutch at Cambridge University before specializing in Dutch poetry for his Ph.D. He also holds a Scandinavian degree in English (Lund) and in German (Odense). He moved to Scandinavia in 1968 and lives at present in Odense, Denmark.

Irons has been active as a translator for almost twenty years, specializing mostly in works to do with art, culture, philosophy, and education. He has also translated considerable quantities of poetry into English, mainly from Dutch and the Scandinavian languages.

The Chinese character for poetry is made up of two parts: "word" and "temple." It also serves as pressmark for Copper Canyon Press.

Since 1972, Copper Canyon Press has fostered the work of emerging, established, and world-renowned poets for an expanding audience. The Press thrives with the generous patronage of readers, writers, booksellers, librarians, teachers, students, and funders—everyone who shares the belief that poetry is vital to language and living.

Major funding has been provided by:

Anonymous (2)
Beroz Ferrell & The Point, LLC
Lannan Foundation
National Endowment for the Arts
Cynthia Lovelace Sears and Frank Buxton
Washington State Arts Commission

For information and catalogs:

COPPER CANYON PRESS
Post Office Box 271
Port Townsend, Washington 98368
360-385-4925
www.coppercanyonpress.org

Copper Canyon Press gratefully acknowledges
Lannan Foundation for supporting the publication and
distribution of exceptional literary works.

LANNAN LITERARY SELECTIONS 2008

Lars Gustafsson, *A Time in Xanadu*

David Huerta, *Before Saying Any of the Great Words: Selected Poetry*

Sarah Lindsay, *Twigs and Knucklebones*

Valzhyna Mort, *Factory of Tears*

Dennis O'Driscoll, *Reality Check*

LANNAN LITERARY SELECTIONS 2000–2007

Maram al-Massri, *A Red Cherry on a White-tiled Floor: Selected Poems,*
translated by Khaled Mattawa

Marvin Bell, *Rampant*

Hayden Carruth, *Doctor Jazz*

Cyrus Cassells, *More Than Peace and Cypresses*

Madeline DeFrees, *Spectral Waves*

Norman Dubie
The Insomniac Liar of Topo
The Mercy Seat: Collected & New Poems, 1967–2001

Sascha Feinstein, *Misterioso*

James Galvin, *X: Poems*

Jim Harrison, *The Shape of the Journey: New and Collected Poems*

Hồ Xuân Hương, *Spring Essence: The Poetry of Hồ Xuân Hương,*
translated by John Balaban

June Jordan, *Directed by Desire: The Collected Poems of June Jordan*

Maxine Kumin, *Always Beginning: Essays on a Life in Poetry*

Ben Lerner, *The Lichtenberg Figures*

Antonio Machado, *Border of a Dream: Selected Poems,*
translated by Willis Barnstone

W.S. Merwin
The First Four Books of Poems
Migration: New & Selected Poems
Present Company

Taha Muhammad Ali, *So What: New & Selected Poems, 1971–2005*,
translated by Peter Cole, Yahya Hijazi, and Gabriel Levin

Pablo Neruda
The Separate Rose, translated by William O'Daly
Still Another Day, translated by William O'Daly

Cesare Pavese, *Disaffections: Complete Poems 1930–1950*,
translated by Geoffrey Brock

Antonio Porchia, *Voices,* translated by W.S. Merwin

Kenneth Rexroth, *The Complete Poems of Kenneth Rexroth*

Alberto Ríos
The Smallest Muscle in the Human Body
The Theater of Night

Theodore Roethke
On Poetry & Craft: Selected Prose of Theodore Roethke
Straw for the Fire: From the Notebooks of Theodore Roethke

Benjamin Alire Sáenz, *Dreaming the End of War*

Rebecca Seiferle, *Wild Tongue*

Ann Stanford, *Holding Our Own: The Selected Poems of Ann Stanford*

Ruth Stone, *In the Next Galaxy*

Joseph Stroud, *Country of Light*

Rabindranath Tagore, *The Lover of God,*
translated by Tony K. Stewart and Chase Twichell

Reversible Monuments: Contemporary Mexican Poetry,
edited by Mónica de la Torre and Michael Wiegers

César Vallejo, *The Black Heralds,* translated by Rebecca Seiferle

Eleanor Rand Wilner, *The Girl with Bees in Her Hair*

Christian Wiman, *Ambition and Survival: Becoming a Poet*

C.D. Wright
One Big Self: An Investigation
Steal Away: Selected and New Poems

Matthew Zapruder, *The Pajamaist*

The font used for this book is Centaur, an old-style serif typeface originally drawn as titling capitals by Bruce Rogers in 1912–14 for the Metropolitan Museum of Art. Book design and composition by Phil Kovacevich. Printed on archival-quality paper at McNaughton & Gunn, Inc.